Contents

Introduction

My name is David Bennett. I have a bachelor's degree in Civil Engineering and reached the rank of Eagle Scout in the Boy Scouts of America. I have three boys and a loving wife, and we live on a large farm with lots of different animals. I have had many jobs in all different areas throughout my life, from laboring in a factory, to painting, to designing residential developments. All of this has led me to where I am today.

I now work as a program manager with a mid-sized company, and my team designs high-voltage power transmission lines for various clients across the country. I started working here in 2009. I am writing this book to explain to the best of my ability my method of managing my team.

It's a simple book. There are no figures or stats. No references to large studies or documented management styles. I am not a Project Management Professional as certified by the Project Management Institute. I haven't even been doing this for a terribly long time. I have received feedback from my superiors and fellow employees that I'm a great manager and want to share what I do.

I decided to write this book in the fashion of an interview, posing questions and providing answers that I hope bring some understanding of how I think and manage. I have added personal stories to back this up. I hope that by reading this you will understand what I have accomplished through my style of management, and maybe it will inspire you to make changes in your own management style.

Why do you love managing?

I love the self-satisfaction of knowing that I'm taking care of my teammates to the best of my ability, making sure they feel productive and accomplished at work and that they are rewarded and appreciated for their efforts.

My goal is to be on a personal level with my teammates and try to help make their lives better. Not just their work lives. Their entire lives. I want them to be the best they can be. Live the best lives they can.

If someone doesn't want to do their job anymore, I don't get angry or beg or try to manipulate them to stay. I'm happy that they were able to look at their life and make a change when needed. I ask them what they want to do, and if I can help them out in any way, I try to do so. If there's something else I think they can do within the company that will excite them, I try to suggest that. And if they do leave, I don't cut them out of my life. I want to stay connected with them and watch them succeed in whatever they do.

I recently had a teammate express to me that they were feeling very stressed and overwhelmed, and it was starting to cause issues outside of work. They were thinking about going into a different career path. I honestly wasn't surprised; I had noticed signs over the past couple of months but was unable to get answers when I brought the subject up. They were an integral part of our team, so it was a huge blow to me and the group they were working with. I tried to work with them to take some of the stress away and even talked about moving them to a different client for a change of pace. In the end, they made the decision to leave, and I'm glad to say that they are happier today.

Helping to make my teammates happy makes me happy and makes me want to come to work. I am truly grateful for the opportunities that my company has given me. The responsibility they have placed on my shoulders to lead and mold my team helps me come to work wanting to do my best every day.

Why do you care so much for your team?

I care for my team because I want them to be happy and successful and go home feeling fulfilled and proud of what they accomplished that day. We spend so much of our time at work, and none of us should have to spend that many hours somewhere we find displeasure. The more connected I can make my team, the better.

Obviously, not every part of the job can be roses and rainbows. It is work. I make sure that everyone has 40 hours and no one needs to work overtime. I make sure that when someone needs help or has an issue, they feel comfortable coming to me or another teammate. My door is always open. I just want everyone to be as happy as they can be.

Making sure that my teammates have everything they need to do their jobs efficiently is a priority. We have multiple screens in our office, stand up desks, comfortable chairs, and ample office equipment and supplies. If someone needs something specific, I try my best to get it for them.

For example, I had several remote teammates whose equipment showed up, but because of supply issues, they only received one of their two monitors. Two monitors are essential to what we do, and I knew they weren't going to be as efficient and would be frustrated. I made sure to check in with our IT department weekly to see where the other monitors were and had them shipped out to my teammates as soon as they were in.

Other teammates have chosen to transition from in-office to remote work, even some who live within minutes of the office. The one thing COVID taught me is that some people can be just as effective at home as they are in the office. If working from home makes someone happy, then I'm all for it.

I don't complain if people want to listen to music while they're working. If whatever they're doing doesn't interfere with the quality or efficiency of their work, I think it brings some happiness to their jobs.

I want my teammates to feel happy and appreciated for what they do and go home feeling good about themselves. I also want them to have time after work to do what they want to do, not work them so hard that they just go home, eat, and go to bed. I strive to be seen as a caring boss who is fair, friendly, and appreciative.

How does your attitude towards the company affect your management style?

My love for my company makes me want to do my best for my teammates every day so they experience the same feelings.

The company I work for now prides itself on being family oriented, which started from the first day in 1988. Over the years, the company has grown from just a handful of people to almost 1000 today. A lot of this growth has been in the last five years.

With the enormous growth, expanding locations across the US, and the introduction of remote workers comes the challenge of keeping the family-oriented work culture alive. I have no doubt that we'll be able to do it, although the focus might need to shift more to department families or team families. If for some reason the family culture changes at the corporate level, I will try my best to maintain and foster it in my team. To me, nothing feels better than not being a cog in a machine.

To foster this feeling, our owner comes to our offices and goes around to visit with everyone. If someone is new, she introduces herself and spends extra time getting to know them. She truly cares about us all and sees us as people, not just a means of making money for her. She wants us to feel like family and takes great strides to show it.

We have an amazing benefits package that goes beyond our extensive medical/dental/vision insurance, 401k, and typical perks like fitness reimbursement. Scholarship contests for our children, AAA membership, education reimbursement, are some of the additional perks that our owner provides. The owner hosts company picnics to gather everyone together and have fun outside of work. She holds year-end reviews where we all gather for a catered lunch and go over the health and achievements of the company. She makes us all feel like we belong, and I want to make sure that feeling translates to each of my teammates.

What tools do you use to complement your management style?

My management style focuses on being engaged with my teammates. I want to know how they are doing and be able to talk freely with them about any subject, and my company provides me with tools to do this better and more efficiently.

The first tool is an office with a door. Having the door open seems trivial, but it shows that I am always available and willing to talk. Nothing says "leave me alone" more than a shut door. That is the opposite of what I want to project. It also allows me to shut the door when a private conversation needs to happen.

We use Microsoft Teams at work, and I find it to be a terrific way to communicate with both in-office and remote employees. The call function works well, and I can share screens and video of myself whenever I want. It keeps a log of past conversations so I can go back and reference things. It works great for team meetings and makes everyone feel connected no matter where they are in the country.

Teams also helps us engage with our clients. Meetings where we can see each other help foster a friendlier work environment. And since our clients are all over the US, we can show them our designs in real time and discuss things and work out issues. This helps us keep our caring relationships with them and get their projects done quicker and more efficiently.

One of my most important tools is a performance management platform called 15Five. It helps me to build relationships with my teammates, identify and solve problems early, show my appreciation for my teammates, and help them grow within the company. I currently use the check-in feature with all of my teammates. The frequency can be adjusted to daily, weekly, bi-weekly, etc., but monthly seems to be working well for us.

The check-in page has a few sections to it. The first allows teammates to score how they're feeling from one to five. This helps me identify when someone is feeling low so I can inquire as to why that is. Maybe it's work related or personal. Either way, I can provide a listening ear and help problem solve.

The next section is for tasks from the previous month and the coming month. Tasks that were assigned from the previous month can be marked complete if finished and comments can be added to ones that are still in progress. Tasks can be carried over to the next month and new ones can be added as needed.

The third section asks a couple of simple questions. The responses let me know if there's anything anyone needs to help them in their job and if there's anything they would like to be recognized for. The recognition part is usually left blank, or they say they don't have anything. It's hard for people to brag on themselves, so I always suggest things they've done in the past month. Eventually, I hope to wear them down so they start to list accomplishments themselves.

The fourth section is for hi-fives. Teammates can give a hi-five, which is a way of telling someone or a group how much you appreciate them or thank them for helping, etc. These can be given out freely and they further promote the appreciation mentality of the company.

The last section is the comment section, where I supply feedback to the team member. I use this opportunity to show my appreciation and supply each person with suggestions on how they can improve and grow inside the company. Issues can be brought up here and suggestions for addressing them can be offered.

Some of the added features that I like are the ability to assign reaction emojis and make comments on specific items. I find that the emojis let people know I've read their responses and care about what they say and do. Comments can make items more interactive, and I can ask follow-up questions where needed. If there's something that I want to save for our biannual 1-on-1s, I can check a box and it's automatically saved for discussion later in the year.

Lastly, my company uses spot awards. If a teammate goes above and beyond in their tasks, I can send my boss a quick description of what they did and how I appreciated it, and he will send them a gift card with that explanation. I am truly grateful that my company recognizes the need to stay connected and in touch with our employees and supplies these awesome tools.

How do you make your team feel appreciated?

I give them praise for their accomplishments through individual recognition, recognition to a group, spot awards, and bragging about them to the client. First, though, I make sure that I'm friendly with all my employees. No one is going to feel appreciated when the person doing the appreciating is a jerk to them.

I attend the group meetings that my three leads have with their teams and make sure to ask how everyone is doing, how their weekends went, and other questions that arise from past conversations. When you genuinely show interest in your team, they feel like more than just a number. More than just a cog in the machine that is only there to make money for you. I make sure to listen and react to what is being worked on by each teammate. If there are challenges, I offer suggestions if the lead asks for it. Showing interest is a way that I show my appreciation.

I use Microsoft Teams to check in with people and see how their days are going. One day, I sent everyone on my team a message in Teams that just said, "I really appreciate you!" Half of them thanked me, while the other half asked why. Because I know all of them and what they do as part of our team, it wasn't hard to produce specific reasons why I appreciated each of them.

Another way I show my appreciation is to take care of their wants and needs promptly. This lets them know that I care about their happiness and want to make their lives easier at work. I don't expect them to struggle through their tasks when there's something out there that I can supply which will make it easier. Similarly, when my teammates request days off, I make sure to review and approve them immediately. If they are giving me their best, I need to be giving them my best as well because I genuinely appreciate what they do for me.

How does having an appreciated team flow down to a happy client?

I find that when my teammates are happy, they produce excellent work on time, and therefore our clients are happy. It's that simple. By not letting my teammates' responsibilities slip, holding them accountable, appreciating what they do, and trying to make their lives at work as easy as possible, I make it possible for them to focus on their tasks and get them done, which makes our clients feel taken care of and happy.

When I make my teammates' lives at work easier and show my appreciation for what they do, they're willing to do whatever it takes to carry out our goals. Because I make sure overtime is limited, they're willing to work those few instances of overtime without question. They know it's only temporary and things will go back to normal once the assignment is complete. That, or they know that I will figure out a way to get them back to their normal schedule, either by rearranging resources or hiring new teammates.

When we have meetings with our clients, they're not dull and business only. Because we are happy and enjoy our jobs, our meetings are fun. We have friendly relationships with our clients. We ask how their weeks are going or their weekends went. We're happy to share with them, and to hear a little about their lives. In turn, our clients feel like we care, because we really do. I can think of nothing worse than working for a client who's all business all the time. What a way to wear down someone until they're no longer enjoying their work.

I have a client who has very specific standards, schedule, and budget for their projects. My team understands all of this and works hard to meet all three with excellent quality and service. Why does my team do this? Because they are rewarded with a competitive salary, they are appreciated on the team, and they want more money and appreciation. They want to succeed and make the client happy. If I am successful in managing my team, this is the result that I should expect.

I want my teammates to be happy, and I show this through my management style of honesty, appreciation, and dedication to them. After all, I'm not the one who does the work for our clients. I don't do the engineering. I don't talk to the client on a daily or weekly basis about the projects we have. I have a very high level of knowledge about our projects, but it's not necessary for me to be in the weeds on all of them. I wouldn't be able to get anything done if that was the case. My job is to make sure that I have a team that works well together and is knowledgeable about our clients' needs. I need my teammates to want to do the best job they can because when they do that, the client gets what they asked for and more.

We have great relationships with all our clients. Some are on a personal level, but all are friendly. We are honest with them the same way I am honest with my team. Through this honesty, we build trust. With trust comes comfort that we can do the jobs they give us under the constraints they dictate. When we deliver consistently, they make sure we have more projects to work on. If my team is happy, they do good work. If they do good work, the client is happy.

The challenging part is how to make the team do good work. There are a lot of pieces to doing good work: Client standards need to be followed in the design. Budget and time constraints need to be met. Checks and reviews must be done to ensure quality. Design practices that are not taught, but rather learned through experience must be implemented. When all of this happens, that's a win for the team. That win needs to be appreciated and recognized at every level, from the manager down to the technician.

Why is it important for your teammates to grow and how do you help them do that?

I feel that stagnation is not good. Some might say that keeping a person where they are makes them great at that job. But most people will get bored, and if they're bored, they could possibly leave to go somewhere else where they can do something different.

I want my teammates to grow in this company. I want technicians to grow into designers, designers into engineers, and engineers into managers. Now, some of these steps may require more than just learning on the job. For example, to advance from designer to engineer requires a degree. Some people are not willing or able to attain one, and I respect that. There are still levels of designer they can reach and work towards if they want, such as senior designer or principal designer.

Some people only want to do one thing. I have a teammate who only wants to do technician work. They have been doing this for 22 years. I ask them every year if they want to do something different, and they do not. I respect this and don't push further. I ask because I want them to know that I care about them, want to see them grow, and ultimately want them to be happy.

Why is it important for my teammates to grow? Because it keeps the group together. If I can grow the group from within, then I don't have to hire the ability I need from outside the company. I don't have to bring in a stranger and place them above my teammates and potentially block their upward momentum. I can instead bring in new, younger technicians and grow them into designers and engineers. This way, they grow from the bottom, learn the team and company culture, learn what is expected in our group, and feel a sense of accomplishment.

If I do have to bring someone in from the outside to fill a gap that I can't promote from within, I make that decision carefully. I don't want to block my employees from advancement. If someone on my team is on track to advance, I might bring in someone two levels above them. That way, the new employee can handle some of the lower responsibilities, but also mentor the teammate below them to do some of the higher responsibilities.

Growing doesn't have to be from technician to designer and so on. It can also be adding responsibilities to their existing position. Watching my people grow within our team is a very rewarding experience for me.

What does pay have to do with your management style?

I think pay is the most important when it comes to happy employees. I find it hard to believe that someone would stick around at a job if they were appreciated but not compensated well. It's just a fact. People need money.

I have provided my teammates with good compensation for the tasks they perform. My boss has helped me achieve this by allowing me to do market analyses to make sure of it. In the few instances where a teammate has come to me and expressed that they are not making enough or are struggling financially, I take this seriously and work on it right away.

I found that because of our growth, often the teammates that we have hired recently are coming in at a higher pay rate than those who have been with me for several years. It's just a matter of how the market is right now for new hires. My boss and I recognized this, looked at all my employees, and tried our hardest to level the playing field. In the end, a well-compensated teammate will feel that they are truly appreciated for what they do and will want to continue to perform for you to the best of their ability.

Why is honesty so important in managing your team?

Honesty is one of the most important aspects of my management style. If I say I'm going to do something, I'm going to do it. If I make a mistake, I'm going to own it. If there's a problem, I'm going to bring it to attention and discuss it. I want to be honest with my team and I expect the same from them.

How can I expect my teammates to be honest with me if I'm not honest with them? I have a teammate who came to me recently and let me know that they were struggling financially due to the inflation that has taken over our country. They were being honest with me in letting me know this, and I told them I would look at their salary and see what I could do. I could have just said that to make them feel better in the moment and then done nothing about it, but then my words wouldn't mean anything to them in the future. Whatever I tell them or promise them later would be met with a "whatever" response because I've made promises in the past and not followed through.

Instead, I looked at their salary and compared it with similar positions in their area. I talked to my boss, and then I found myself doing the same for all my teammates. In the end, I was able to get the individual a sizeable raise as well as several others on my team. Now whenever this teammate needs something or asks me to do something for them, they know I will do it. I expect that when I ask them to do something for me, they will do it as well. I treat all my teammates with this same honesty and willingness to do what I can to fulfill their requests of me. I expect the same from them, and so far, I have always gotten it.

There is honesty in action and then there is honesty in life. I am very honest about my life to my teammates. I don't make up stories or bend the truth when talking to them. If I'm having a bad day, I let them know. I want them to see that I am just like them and not some superhuman. If someone comes to me with an issue, I am honest in my discussion with them. If I have experience with the issue, I share honestly about how I dealt with it. If I don't know, I tell them that and suggest who they might talk to about it. I certainly don't make something up to seem like I have all the answers because I definitely don't. But I will do whatever I can to help my teammates with whatever issues they have and expect the same from them.

How much do you open up to your teammates about your personal life?

I am an open book. I've had so many experiences in my life and have learned so much that it would be a shame for me to keep that to myself.

I want to know my teammates personally, not just professionally. In order to do that, I need to be open and share about my weekends, what I did after work, what I'm struggling with, and what I have achieved. I cannot ask my teammates to share their personal lives with me without first sharing my own. I let them know that I really do care about them when I listen intently and engage with them. I make sure to give them my undivided attention and keep track of things they're doing so I can follow up with them later.

Now, we don't hang out together outside of work. I'm a busy man and have my own things to do when I get home. But I am interested in what they are interested in. Who knows, someone might do something cool that I might want to experience or have a solution to a problem that I'm struggling with.

I have a teammate who I talk to every day. We discuss things outside of work and share our personal achievements and struggles. We give each other advice when needed to help solve problems we're having. This teammate, being older than I, has had a lot of experience with home repairs and homes in general since they used to be a contractor. If something is going wrong with the house or I need to know how to fix something, I ask for their help. They're always willing to share their knowledge and can usually give me the solution I need quickly. I'm not able to offer them as much advice, but I am able to listen intently and ask questions, which usually leads to them figuring it out on their own. It's a great relationship which I hope our team experiences with me.

Personal conversations also lighten the mood. A lot of people think seeing their boss is stressful. I do not want that. When I need to talk to someone, I always start out with light conversation first. It helps if I have to discuss something difficult to be seen not as a boss, but more of a teammate who is trying to help them succeed. Opening up lets my teammates see me as a person and not just a boss. They see that not everything is rosy with me all the time. I have problems like they do and appreciate their suggestions for how to deal with those problems.

Why are the personal issues so important to solve?

Personal issues carry over into work and can cause a teammate to be less effective at their job. But I'm not looking at this from a money standpoint, I'm looking at it from a happiness standpoint. If someone has something personal going on in their life, they won't be able to focus, will be frustrated or angry or sad, and most likely distracted. I don't want that. I want my teammates to come to work happy and able to focus on the tasks at hand.

Sure, there are going to be issues at work, but I think it's easier for people to let go of those once they leave the office. On the other hand, it's almost impossible to let go of personal issues when you get to work.

I find that people are more likely to open up to me when I share my personal struggles with them. I open up, and then they do as well. I can make suggestions based on my past experiences. And if I don't have any past experiences, I can at least listen. Often times, I learn how to solve my own issues because one of my teammates has had the same problem and tells me how they solved it.

I want my teammates to know that I care about them, not just when they are here at work. I care about them completely and will do whatever I can to make sure that they are as happy as they can be.

How do you predict what your teammates are going to worry about and calm their fears?

With every job, there are ebbs and flows. This can be daily, monthly, or yearly. Job security is essential to my teammates and is something I know they worry about from time to time.

The way my team is set up, we have three main clients. One might be swamped with work while another is normal, and the other is light. My teammates are able to shift clients with ease whenever possible. We have good relationships with our clients, so if we are seeing a slowdown in work, we can talk to them about it and see what's going on and when we can expect things to pick up again.

I recently hired a new project manager to replace someone on my team who left. Not long after we brought them in, it seemed like our workload started to dry up. I knew they were seeing this and were concerned about their future here. I made it a point to talk to them about what was going on. To let them know that their job was not in jeopardy. We talked about our plans for the future and how we would try to get more work.

I was able to keep them busy with the work that we had at the time and get them introduced to other clients to start building those relationships. I took their suggestions on how to get more work and helped them go after those ideas. They have been successful in getting us hooked up with a new client who has promised a good bit of work for us, and they will be running that show.

Over my years of managing, I have learned the ability to empathize with a multitude of situations. This lets me step into my teammates' shoes and try to see what they're worrying about. Whether that's job security, money, or job growth, I can then focus on those worries and communicate how I'm working to resolve them. I want my people to be comfortable at work and not have to worry about something we can control if we look at it early enough.

How do you make sure that you're not being taken advantage of?

When I was head beach guard, I used to do all the tasks that no one else wanted to do. I was constantly weed eating the beach area, picking up trash, cleaning the restrooms, and picking up goose poop. I wanted my employees to be happy but didn't know how to do that properly. Because of that, my employees got to do whatever they wanted while I worked away. They were happy, but I wasn't being a fair manager.

Today I make sure I have expectations for all my teammates and that they know and can meet those expectations. As long as they take care of their responsibilities, I will be as nice and accommodating as I can. When I start to see those responsibilities slip or go off track, I have a discussion with the teammate about how we can get it back in the right direction.

I rarely ask more of my teammates, but never ask less. It's a good understanding that we have, and they know that it allows me to do my best for them.

How do you deal with problems with a team member?

A problem with a team member is also a problem with me. I approach the individual in a face-to-face meeting or Teams call if remote and pose the issue as one that *we* have. I let them know that I want to help solve it and that they are not in trouble.

It's easy for me to understand the problems they face since I have done everything that I ask my teammates to do at one point or another in my career at this company. I might not be up to date on the latest way of doing things, but I make sure that I understand the problem we are facing so I can give good, honest advice. I certainly do not yell or raise my voice. That only brings conflict or makes the person clam up and not share what I need them to share.

I want to have a calm, frank discussion with them so we both understand what the problem is, how it is affecting the team, and how we can solve it. When caught early enough, it requires only a discussion and is usually lighthearted. I will follow up a couple of days later to see how the solution is working and if we need to discuss anything else.

If the problem persists, we have another discussion with HR and implement a Performance Improvement Plan. This is just a way of documenting the problem and proposed solution and starts the paper trail in the unfortunate event that termination is reached. I have been lucky to not have to fire anyone, though I have done some Performance Improvement Plans and placed some individuals on suspension.

I had a teammate who was not producing the expected quality of work and was causing their teammates to pick up the slack. I had a discussion with them to talk about the issue and possible solutions. Weeks later, the problem was still present. This time, I brought their supervisor in with them and discussed the issue in more detail. We discovered that this teammate was not fully trained on the tasks they were being asked to perform. We wrote up a Performance Improvement Plan that detailed the issue and documented the solution, which was for the teammate to receive training. Follow up discussions were held to see if there was improvement, and slowly, we saw progress. This teammate is now more capable and is able to handle the tasks they are given. If they need training on something, they ask and receive what they need.

Now, this only works for what I would consider minor issues. Obviously if there is something serious like harassment, violence, etc., we follow a different path. It's good to be familiar with your company's policies in case you ever need to use them. I have a team works well together, and everyone respects everyone else. It's particularly important to treat everyone the same. Do not play favorites. This only leads to more issues down the line and will erode the team quickly.

How do you motivate your team?

The ultimate motivator is money. If you have unlimited funds, you can motivate anyone to do anything. Unfortunately, I do not have unlimited funds.

How do I motivate people, then? First, I make sure they are fairly compensated. It's hard to motivate someone if they're not being paid at or close to market value.

We also have a performance-driven bonus at our company. I will say that it seems low compared to larger businesses, but you have to consider all the benefits that my company provides to everyone. Our owner provides us with lots of additional benefits such as AAA membership, Executive Costco membership upgrades, education reimbursement, scholarship contests for our kids. The list goes on. We are truly fortunate when it comes to the benefit package.

I use spot rewards for outstanding service. These are $100 gift cards and are given out by my boss. I provide him with the reasoning why a teammate deserves one, and if he agrees, will hand them out.

Every couple of months, I buy the in-office team lunch.

What I have unlimited amounts of is appreciation. I'm always letting my teammates know how appreciative I am of them. It doesn't matter how small the task is, I make sure to let them know that I appreciate their effort.

I supply a challenging environment for my people to work in. The projects we get are interesting and varied. I work to make sure our technicians are learning the design, the designers are learning the engineering, and the engineers are learning to lead and manage. Through growth comes more money. And more money is a great motivator.

How has having remote teammates affected how you manage?

Having remote teammates has been a challenge to me for sure. Up to this point in my life, I've always been able be in the same room as my employees. I've been able to do things for them like take them to lunch, shake their hands, and talk face to face with them. Not so anymore.

I have people all over the country working on my team. Great people whom I have good relationships with and who do great things for the team. I might never get to meet these people in person, though I hope that someday I will. For the time being, I use the tools that are given to me to manage them.

I use Microsoft Teams to communicate with them and see their faces. I use 15Five to check in on how they're doing. I talk to them, not about work, but just personally to nurture the connection I have with them. I look for opportunities to recognize them and show my appreciation.

I am constantly thinking of ways to give them the same sort of experience that my in-office teammates have. Some of my thoughts thus far have been to send them money to buy their lunch on days when I get lunch for the in-office folks. I will have more Teams meetings so everyone is on the same level, and no one is getting preferential treatment. I will work with my company and suggest ways that we can include our remote workers in the extra benefits that the in-office people have.

One perk that comes to mind is the annual summer picnic we have for the folks near one of our main offices. I feel bad when I see emails going out to everyone talking about the picnics, knowing that I have a person on my team who won't get to take part because they live too far away. How can we include them?

Some will say that being remote has drawbacks that just come with the situation. This is true to some extent, but it doesn't have to be for everything. Maybe they can't get together with a large group of coworkers and spend a day together at a picnic, but that doesn't mean we can't talk to the person and find out what special event they would like to partake in and purchase that for them. Maybe that's a ticket to a theme park or a nice dinner out.

One example of how our company has been more inclusive of remote workers is our Christmas giveaways. In the past, we would have company Christmas parties where gifts were raffled off for those who attended. This doesn't work for our remote employees, so our HR department made a change. Instead of giving away gifts at the parties, they started doing online games that everyone could take part in. For twelve days, the HR team has quizzes, games, and contests, and the winners get increasingly better gifts as the days go on. Ideas like this help everyone feel a part of the family and appreciated.

How do you interview people so you're getting a good fit for the team you want?

When I interview someone, the first and most important thing I focus on is how well I connect with them. I know that if I connect with them, they're also going to connect with my team. Why do I know this? Because I know how I connect with my team. I know how they relate to me and to each other.

When I interview someone, I ask them how they're doing. I ask them how their week is going, if they did anything interesting over the weekend. I try to get them talking about their personal life. I share information about my life and use this to get them started if they're hesitant. I ask them about their family and tell them about mine. I try to connect with them personally. Depending on how much they take part and their answers, I can figure out how well they'll fit into my team.

Second is the skills and experiences I'm looking for. It's a close second, but I figure I can always train the person to be better qualified for the position. They will not be able to learn and grow, though, if they don't connect with the team on a friendly, personal level. My team won't want to work with them or engage with them if there's not a personal connection. The team would ultimately have to work together, but they wouldn't enjoy it and it would become a sore spot and cause disharmony.

Connecting on a personal level also lets the candidate know who I am and what sort of team they should expect to join. Some people might not like my team dynamic, and that's fine. It's not for everyone. My team is broken into three groups, and each group is unique. When I'm interviewing, I'm trying to fill a particular position in one of these groups. I not only have to make sure that the candidate is a good fit for the team as a whole, but also for the group they'll be in. I'm not going to put an older person who is nearing retirement and wants to coast for a couple of years in with my group of driven young individuals no matter how qualified that person is. Everything needs to fit and be in harmony.

Why do you focus on your team and not other things like revenue and profit?

Don't get me wrong, I focus on revenue and profit. I wouldn't have a job if I didn't. I just spend more time focusing on my team because it's my team that makes the revenue and profit possible.

My team works on a time and material basis for about 95% of our work. This means that the only way I can increase my revenue is by increasing my team size or by making them work more hours. I don't want to make my team work more hours because that leads to burnout and unhappy people. I therefore need to grow the size of my team.

Ideally, I want to do that from within. Whenever possible, I would rather grow my teammates into those gaps than bring in outside hires. I would be very angry if an outside hire took the job I was hoping to be promoted into. I would think that my boss didn't care about me or my advancement in my career. I want to hire the lower levels. I want to hire someone who starts at the bottom and works their way up.

If my team is happy, then they do good work. If they do good work, then the client is happy. If the client is happy, then they give us more work. If they give us more work, then I need to hire more people to do the work. If I have more people working for me, then my revenue grows. When my revenue grows, the amount of profit that I make grows. It is a simple process that has yet to fail me.

How long have you been managing this way?

I guess I've been trying to manage this way since I was head beach guard at a lake in Ohio back in 1997. I wanted my employees to like me more than anything back then, so I would often do the tasks that no one else wanted to do instead of managing my team in a fair manner.

My second management opportunity was ten years later, and again I didn't do very well. I was a project manager and found myself overwhelmed with making sure projects were kept under budget and on time. I didn't focus on making sure my team was taken care of. My team did not work well together, we were over budget a lot, and ultimately, I was let go when the market took a dive. That all changed when I got to my current job.

The company I work for now has a goal of being family oriented, which suits me well. Even though we are growing at a good pace, the family style is still front and center. I started to find that if my team was happy, trained properly, and appreciated, the money took care of itself. It really kicked off once I started hiring managers under me who had the same approach and could help make sure everything was going smoothly.

I think I'm in a good groove now with my style. It hasn't proven me wrong in the last eight years. Because of my company's family orientation, our retention rate is extremely high. This helps immensely because everyone has been working together for years and knows each other well. I can see how the team works and bring in new people who will fit into that system.

Why is your team the best in the company?

Because I say that they are, and tell them often, and believe that it is true. So far, they have not proven me wrong!

Everyone is willing to help each other out. Everyone is willing to stay late if the situation calls for it in order to get a job done. Everyone understands that our team's success is dependent on our individual successes.

My teammates want to learn our clients and do a great job for them. No one on our team is just doing the bare minimum to get the job done. We follow the processes and procedures set by our company in regard to safety, quality, and training. We don't settle for where we are. We are constantly looking to improve.

We have quality audits on completed projects where we go over the entire project with the auditor and cover everything from when the kickoff meeting was held to what forms were used to track deliverables, to how many mistakes were caught before the job was sent to the client. We ask questions during these audits to make sure we are keeping up with the procedures set by the company and talk about where we can improve if we're not meeting them. I like to think that we are one of the happiest groups in the company and that I help make that so.

Conclusion

I hope that this has supplied some insight into how I manage my team and the results that I get. Like I mentioned in the beginning, there are no studies referenced or charts full of data. I have provided my personal thoughts and experiences. I have not been doing this for a long time, but I have seen great results so far with my approach. I am greatly appreciative to my team and company for giving me the successes that I have achieved. I would not be able to do what I do today without them.